Straight Forward with Science

LIFE CYCLES

Peter Riley

To my granddaughter, Tabitha Grace.

Published in paperback in Great Britain in 2018 by The Watts Publishing Group

Editor: Julia Bird
Designer: Mo Choy Design

ISBN 978 1 4451 3552 6
Library ebook ISBN 978 1 4451 3551 9
Dewey number: 591.56

Picture acknowledgements: amenic 181/Shutterstock: 6t. Petrov Anton/Shutterstock: 17t. Art Family/Shutterstock: 22t. Kitch Bain/Shutterstock: 20b, 31. Bonnie Taylor Barrie/Shutterstock: 8b. blickwinkel/Hartl/Alamy: 29t. Blue Ring Media/Shutterstock: 6b. Steve Byland/Shutterstock: 29b. Catfish Photography/Shutterstock: front cover, 1, 4t. chmelars/Dreamstime: 24l. Adi Cinrea/Shutterstock: 24r. dbdavidova/Shutterstock: 23b. Dennis W Donohue/Shutterstock: 25b. Wim Van Egmond/Visuals Unlimited Inc/SPL: 26t. Elena Elisseeva/Shutterstock: 7t. Enigmangels/Shutterstock 9t. Dirk Erchen /Shutterstock: 17b. Famveld/Shutterstock: 27b. Vladislav Gajic/Dreamstime: 22b. Nic Hamilton/Alamy: 16b. happykamil/Shutterstock: 14c. Hellem/Dreamstime: 26b. Rob Holdor/Shutterstock: 16t. ISM/SPL: 21t. ivancreative/Shutterstock: 7b. Attila Jandi/Shutterstock: 15t. Jeka 84/Shutterstock: 25t. Mirek Kijewski/Shutterstock: 2, 12t, 13c. Koo/Shutterstock: 28b. KPE_Payless/Shutterstock: 5t. Andrey_Kuzmin/Shutterstock: 21b. Carsten Medom Madsen/Shutterstock: 9b. Maksimilian/Shutterstock: 11b. Anastaiia Malinich/Shutterstock: 10c. Martchaa/Shutterstock: 3t, 3b, 19b. nito/Shutterstock: 10t. Claude Nuridsany & Marie Perennou/SPL: 13t. Alexander Ozerov/Shutterstock: 19t. Phillip Palton/Alamy: 12b. William Perugini/Shutterstock: 23t. Pniesen/Dreamstime: 27t. Prentiss40/Dreamstime: 19c. Reddogs/Dreamstime: 18l. Reika/Shutterstock: 10b. Qui Ju Song/Shutterstock: 4b. Max Sudakov/Shutterstock: 5b. Jack Sullivan/Alamy: 29c. Survivalphotos/Alamy: 14b. Tomo/Shutterstock: 15b. Twilight Art Pictures/Shutterstock: 11t. Vasily Vishnevsky/Shutterstock: 18br. CC. Wikipedia: 28t. worldswildlifewonders/Shutterstock: 20t.

Printed in China

Franklin Watts
An imprint of
Hachette Children's Group
Part of The Watts Publishing Group
Carmelite House
50 Victoria Embankment
London EC4Y 0DZ

An Hachette UK Company
www.hachette.co.uk

www.franklinwatts.co.uk

Contents

Animal and plant life cycles

Every living thing has a life cycle. This is the series of stages in its life as it grows and develops, from the beginning of its life until its death. A life cycle can be as short as a few weeks or as long as two hundred years.

STAGES IN A LIFE CYCLE

There are similar stages in the life cycle of plants and animals. They all have a young, growing stage. At this time they increase in size and become fully formed. The next stage is the mature stage. The mature plant and animal can now reproduce. At the end of the mature stage, the living thing enters a period of old age. In old age the organs of its body fail to work as well as in earlier stages. Eventually the life cycle ends when the plant or animal dies.

Elephant herds include both young and old. The herd is led by an older female of sixty years of age or more.

ANIMAL LIFE CYCLES

The life cycle of most animals starts when an egg is laid. The life cycle of mammals begins when the baby mammal is born. Some young animals look like miniature adults and simply get bigger as they grow. Many insects and all amphibians have a complete change of form called metamorphosis as they go through their life cycle.

These ladybirds have hatched from eggs.

EPHEMERALS

The first stage in a flowering plant's life cycle is the seed. After the seed germinates (sprouts), the plant grows. Some plants grow quickly, mature early, make flowers, fruits and seeds, then die in just a few weeks. These plants are called ephemerals. Many weed plants are ephemerals.

These shepherd's purse plants are ephemerals. The top of the stalk still has flowers, while lower down the flowers have produced fruits.

Oak trees can take up to 50 years to produce fruits called acorns.

ANNUALS, BIENNIALS AND PERENNIALS

Plants that complete their life cycle in a year are called annuals. Other plants take two years to complete their life cycle. They grow roots and leaves in the first year and flowers in the second. They are called biennials. Many plants are perennials. They live for many years, producing flowers and fruit every year. Herbaceous plants can be annuals, biennials or perennials. Woody plants such as conifers and flowering plants that grow as trees and bushes are perennials.

INVESTIGATE

What life cycle stages can you see in the plants and animals you have at home or at school?

Pollinating plants

The first stage in the life cycle of a flowering plant is the seed. When the seed receives enough water and warmth, it germinates.

SEEDLING

First, a root grows out of the seed to find more water from the soil. Next, a shoot grows up out of the seed to find light. The plant at this stage is called a seedling. The leaves use the energy in light, carbon dioxide from the air and water and minerals from the soil to make food for the plant in a process called photosynthesis.

The shoot of a seedling grows above ground and begins to use the energy in sunlight to make food.

READY TO REPRODUCE

As the seedling grows, it forms more roots and leaves. Eventually it becomes mature and opens its flowers. It is now ready to reproduce. The first stage in reproduction is pollination. There are two kinds of pollination – animal pollination and wind pollination.

FLOWERS AND POLLINATION

Flowers play an important part in pollination. Animal-pollinated plants have flowers with colourful petals that produce scent to attract insects. The flowers of wind-pollinated plants do not have petals and are usually green. Both types of flower have stamens. The stamen has a stalk called a filament with a swollen tip called the anther which makes pollen. Both types of flower also have at least one ovary at the centre of the stamens. A stalk called the style grows out of the top of the ovary. At the tip of the style is a sticky surface called the stigma.

stigma
anther
stamen
style
filament
petal
sepal
ovary

The parts of an animal-pollinated flowering plant

The ragweed plant produces lots of pollen. It relies on the wind to spread its pollen far and wide.

WIND POLLINATION

Pollination occurs when the pollen from the anther of one flower travels to the stigma of another flower of the same kind. Wind-pollinated flowers hang out their stamens so that their lightweight, smooth pollen can fall into the air currents and be carried along by the wind to the stigmas of other flowers.

ANIMAL POLLINATION

Most flowers are pollinated by insects such as bees, though some are pollinated by birds or bats. Pollination happens when animals visit pollinated flowers for nectar. The nectar is made at the base of the petals so the animals have to squeeze past the stamens to reach it. The pollen of these flowers has a spiky surface that makes it stick to the animal's hairy body as they pass by. Later, when the animal visits other flowers of the same kind of plant, the pollen sticks to the new plant's stigma.

INVESTIGATE

How many different kinds of animal- and wind-pollinated plants are in flower in a habitat near your home or school? Can you find out what they are called?

A bee picks up pollen on its hairy body as it searches for nectar in flowers.

Fertilisation and fruits

Each pollen grain carries inside it a cell, called a male gamete. It contains half the instructions for making a new plant. When the pollen grain lands on a stigma it grows a tube down the style into the ovary and the male gamete goes down it.

FERTILISATION

In the ovary is at least one ovule. This contains a cell, called the female gamete. It contains another half of the instructions for making a new plant. The male gamete leaves the pollen tube and fuses with the female gamete in a process called fertilisation. The two sets of instructions join together and set about turning the ovule into a seed so that a new plant can grow.

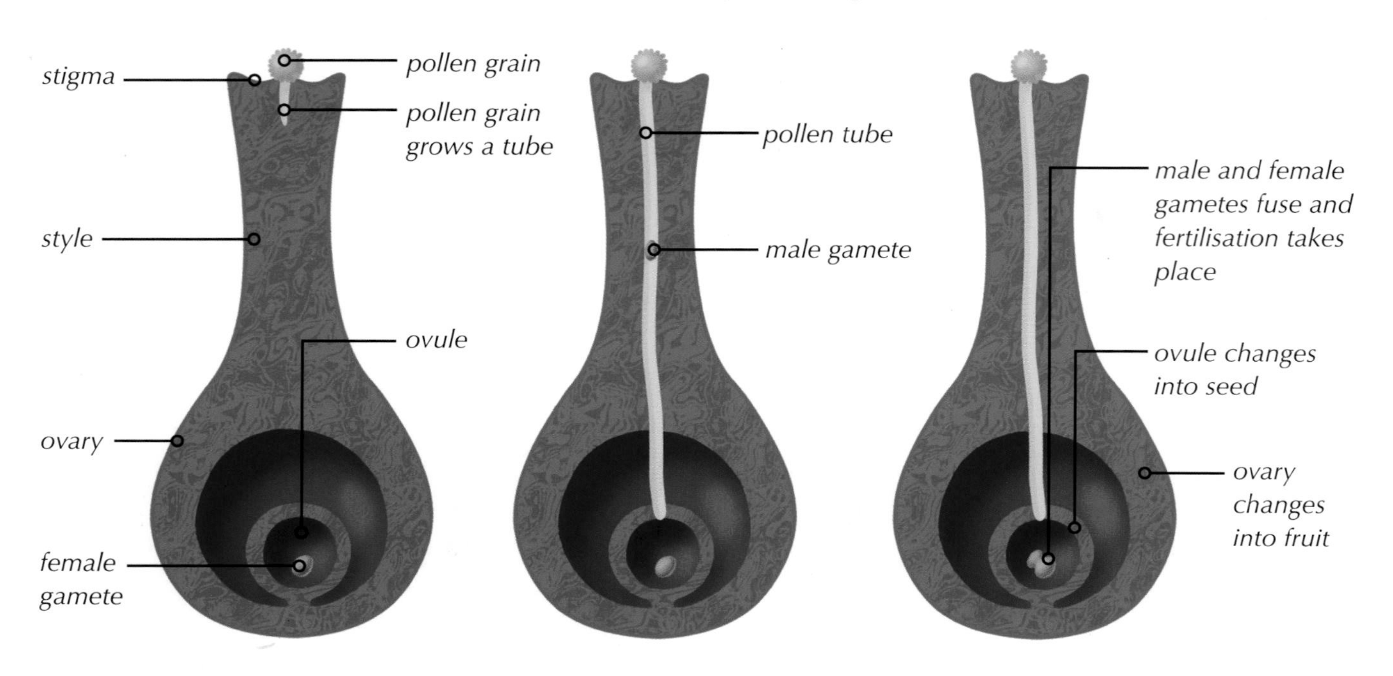

FORMING FRUITS

As seeds form in the ovary, the petals and stamens of the flower fall away and the ovary turns into a fruit. The purpose of the fruit is to disperse the plant's seeds. In some plants the walls of the ovary become thick and watery. They form brightly coloured juicy fruits that attract animals to eat them. Inside the animal's body the walls of the fruit are digested, but the seeds are unharmed. They eventually pass out of the animal with its droppings and can begin to germinate. Some plants form fruits which have a hard woody outer wall around them. We call these fruits nuts. Animals such as squirrels store them for a winter food supply, but forget where they put some of them. These forgotten nuts grow into new plants.

These bright, juicy berries attract lots of birds.

This horse has spiky fruits in its mane.

SPIKY FRUITS

Many plants produce fruits with dry walls. Some of these fruits, such as those of the burdock plant, grow spikes that stick to the fur or feathers of passing animals. They are pulled away from the plant as the animal moves on. Later, the fruits fall to the ground where the seeds can germinate.

FLYING AWAY

The dry walls of fruits such as the sycamore and maple form wings, while plants such as the dandelion and the willow herb form parachutes. Both these structures catch the wind and carry away the seeds. A few fruits have walls that twist as they dry, then break open – shooting out their seeds in all directions!

INVESTIGATE

Look for plants forming fruits around your home and school. Which type of fruit is the most common?

When these winged sycamore fruits fall from the tree they spin in the air and are blown away by the wind.

New plants from old

The type of reproduction where male and female gametes join to make a new plant is called sexual reproduction. Many plants can reproduce without sexual reproduction, which means they only need one parent. This is called asexual reproduction. The new plants form from part of the parent plant and grow up to be identical to it.

Lots of small bulbs have grown from the buds on the flat stem of this garlic bulb.

A side bud on this crocus corm has started to grow into a new plant.

BULBS

Some plants reproduce asexually from bulbs. A bulb is formed from a flat circular stem with tightly packed leaves growing on top of it. These leaves are swollen with food. Between the leaves are buds which sprout from the stem. The leaves use their stored food to grow up out of the soil and make food using sunlight. Over time, some of this food is used to make the buds grow into small bulbs which separate from the parent bulb. Garlic, onions and daffodils grow from bulbs.

CORMS

A corm is a short thick stem that grows underground. Buds sprout out from the corm. One or more of these can change into a new corm. The crocus and the Chinese water chestnut produce corms to reproduce asexually.

RHIZOME

A rhizome is a thick underground stem that grows horizontally under the ground. Buds on the stem can grow into more rhizomes which spread out from the parent stem. Ginger plants and bamboo grow rhizomes.

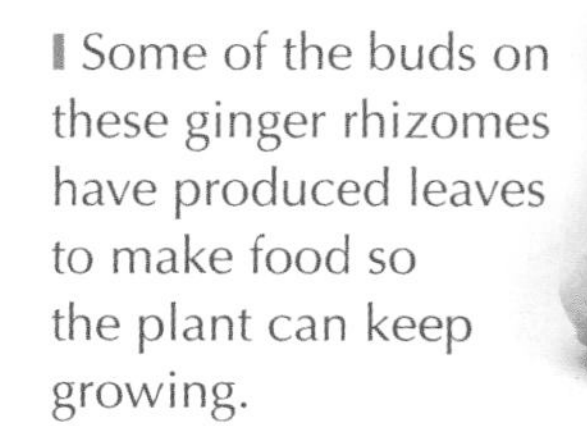

Some of the buds on these ginger rhizomes have produced leaves to make food so the plant can keep growing.

The buds on these potatoes have started to sprout and are ready to grow into new plants.

TUBER

The potato plant can reproduce asexually. It sends out long thin stems in all directions and uses parts of them to store food. The stored food makes the stem swell up into a tuber. The 'eyes' on a potato are really buds. Each one can grow into a new plant. Some gardeners let potato eyes sprout and then cut up the potatoes into pieces, each with a sprouting eye. When these are planted each one grows into a new potato plant.

RUNNERS

Some plants, such as strawberry plants, grow long thin stems, called runners, from their main stem. The runners grow over the ground and new plants grow from their buds.

INVESTIGATE

Separate the small bulbs in a garlic bulb and plant them in a tray of compost. Keep the compost moist and put the tray in a warm, sunny place. Record the growth of each bulb.

The runners from strawberry plants spread out and produce new plants all around them.

The life cycle of a desert locust

Some insects have three stages to their life cycles – egg, nymph and adult. The desert locust is an example of an insect with this life cycle.

The desert locust is a species of grasshopper that is found in parts of Africa, Asia and the Middle East.

SWARMING LOCUSTS

The desert locust lives in desert and scrub habitats. When the male and female locusts are fully grown, they seek out each other to mate. Locusts usually live in small groups, but sometimes they form a huge group called a swarm. Mating takes place in the groups or swarms. After the eggs are fertilised the female seeks out a place to lay them.

A swarm of locusts can very quickly cause great damage to a field of crops.

Desert locust eggs.

FROM EGG TO NYMPH

The desert locust's eggs are laid in a hole in the sand. Between eighty and a hundred eggs are laid together. If the weather is warm the eggs hatch after about two weeks, but if it is cold it may take up to ten weeks. When the eggs hatch the nymphs climb out of the hole and begin to feed. They look like miniature adults, but they do not have wings.

This desert locust has made its final moult and left its old skin behind (left).

FROM NYMPH TO ADULT

The nymphs begin feeding on plants. Over the course of about 35 days they moult five times as they grow. By the fourth moult the wings are almost fully formed.

ADULT LIFE

After a fifth moult, the nymph turns into an adult. The adults feed on the same plants as the nymphs. Part of the food they eat is used to develop the sex organs to make eggs and sperm. It takes the adult usually between two and four months of feeding to become mature and able to breed. The life span of a desert locust varies. In warm conditions with plenty of food it may only be three months, but in cooler conditions it can be five months or more.

INVESTIGATE

Find out about other types of insect with a similar life cycle to the locust. They include cockroaches, stick insects, grasshoppers, crickets, dragonflies, earwigs and praying mantids. Use books and the Internet to find out about the details of their life cycle.

The life cycle of a butterfly

Most insects have a life cycle that is divided into four stages: egg, larva (caterpillar), pupa (or chrysalis) and adult. The butterfly is an example of an insect with this life cycle.

▮ This tree nymph butterfly is laying her fertilised eggs on the underside of a leaf to keep them safe.

EGG

The larva of a butterfly can only feed on certain kinds of plant. This means a female must seek these plants out, then lay her eggs on them. The eggs are usually laid on the underside of a leaf to hide them from predators. The eggs usually hatch in about two weeks, but some butterflies hibernate through the winter in the egg stage and hatch the following spring.

LARVA

When the larvae or caterpillars are ready to hatch they eat their way through the egg shell. Most caterpillars keep on eating the egg shell for a while, then move on to the food plant. As the caterpillar feeds, it grows by moulting. A caterpillar may moult up to seven times and become two hundred times heavier than when it hatched.

▮ A caterpillar has three pairs of legs close to its mouth and five pairs of limbs called prolegs along its body to help it move.

This tree nymph butterfly has recently emerged from its protective pupa.

PUPA

The pupa forms from the last moult of the fully grown caterpillar. The skin of the pupa forms a protective case in which the caterpillar changes into an adult butterfly. Butterflies can take only a few days to pupate in spring and summer, but in autumn they may hibernate as a pupa until the following year so the young they produce will grow up in the warmer weather of spring.

INVESTIGATE

Do caterpillars prefer to feed on one side of a bush? Place a white sheet beneath the south-facing side of a leafy, non-evergreen bush, then shake its branches and observe the caterpillars that fall on the sheet. Repeat with north, east and west facing sides. Be sure to return the fallen insects to the bush.

Adult butterflies feed on nectar from plants.

ADULT BUTTERFLY

The adult emerges by breaking out of the pupa, then stretches and dries its wings before flying away to find food and a mate. The life span of a butterfly varies with species. Some small adult butterflies only live for a week, while larger butterflies may live for a month or even more.

The life cycle of a frog

A frog is an amphibian. All amphibians have a stage in their life cycle during which they grow and develop in water. This is followed by the adult stage when they may live on land, but return to the water to breed.

Frogs lay eggs to reproduce. The eggs are coated in jelly to make it difficult for predators to eat them. They stick together to form frog spawn.

EGG TO TADPOLE

Adult frogs live in damp habitats on land, but in the spring they gather in ponds to mate. The female releases hundreds of eggs into the water and the male releases sperm onto them. Fertilisation takes place in the water. This process is called external fertilisation. The egg develops into a tadpole in about three weeks. When the tadpole hatches it clings to a plant for two days while its mouth and external gills develop fully. As soon as it can open its mouth, it feeds on the algae that coats water plants.

THE DEVELOPING TADPOLE

In the following weeks the tadpole's body and tail become fully shaped and its eyes and nostrils take a more adult form. The external gills are absorbed into the body and the tadpole breathes with internal gills. The tadpole is a herbivore at this time. On its underside it has a long, coiled intestine which helps to digest plant food.

gills

This tadpole still has external gills to take up oxygen dissolved in the water

MEAT-EATER

By two months of age the tadpole develops lungs and comes to the water's surface to breathe. Two buds form at the base of its tail, which eventually grow into back legs. The tadpole changes into a carnivore and begins to feed on insect larvae. It may also feed on smaller tadpoles and the flesh of dead animals such as snails. Its intestine becomes shorter as its diet changes.

INVESTIGATE

Find out about the life cycle of the midwife toad and frogs that live in bromeliad plants.

A frog has large eyes to look for prey and a large mouth to catch them.

FROM TADPOLE TO FROG

Between three and four months of age the tadpole grows front legs and its tail is absorbed into its body. Its small mouth is replaced by a wider one. The tadpole becomes a tiny frog around 12 weeks after hatching. It takes four years for the frog to grow into a mature adult that can breed. Frogs usually live for around eight years.

The crested newt lives in water in the larval stage of its life cycle.

OTHER AMPHIBIANS

Other animals in the amphibian group that share this life cycle include toads, newts, salamanders and worm-like creatures called caecilians that live in wet tropical regions. A few amphibians such as the mudpuppy stay in water all their lives, while the axolotl may stay as a tadpole and even reproduce in that stage.

The life cycle of a starling

There are just over ten and a half thousand different species of birds, but they all have a similar life cycle. The starling is a species of bird. It is found in Europe, North America and Australia.

BREEDING

To reproduce, the male starling must first attract a female. He does this in the spring by singing and by building part of a nest using grass, straw and leaves. Starling nests are usually found in holes in trees and buildings. After a female joins the male starling, she lines the nest with soft materials such as moss and feathers. During this time mating takes place. The female lays up to six eggs and keeps them warm (incubates them).

This male starling is singing to attract a mate.

INSIDE THE EGG

Inside each egg is a tiny embryo. It is held onto the side of a large sphere which provides all the food for the growth of the chick. After about 12 days of incubation, a starling chick is fully formed. It hatches by pecking at the inside of the shell to make a hole, then climbs out.

A clutch of starling eggs in their nest.

NESTLING

A chick in its nest is called a nestling. The starling nestling has bare skin at first, then grows a fuzzy grey down to keep warm. Both parents share the responsibility of feeding the chicks on a diet of worms and soft insects. Soon the nestling begins to grow feathers. After three weeks a nestling's feathers are almost complete. It leaves the nest and becomes known as a fledgling.

Parent starlings feed their chicks insects.

This juvenile starling has grown its winter plumage (see below).

FLEDGLING

The fledgling's feathers continue to grow as it learns to fly and follows its parent to be fed. The parents continue to feed the fledgling for up to two weeks. By that time the fledgling has learnt how to feed itself and is now known as a juvenile.

GROWING UP

The juvenile starling has a dull grey plumage, but after about two months it moults. Its new plumage for the winter has pale spots. The following year the starling moults again. This time it grows a full adult plumage and is ready to breed. An adult starling usually lives for around two to three years.

INVESTIGATE

Using other books and the Internet, find out about some different bird life cycles, such as penguins, ostriches or parrots.

In autumn and winter starlings gather together in huge flocks.

Life cycles of mammals

There are three groups of mammals – egg-laying mammals (montremes), marsupials and placental mammals. They each have different life cycles.

EGG-LAYING MAMMALS

There are three kinds of egg-laying mammal. Two are species of spiny anteater, but the most famous is the duck-billed platypus. After a male and female platypus have mated, the female builds a burrow under the ground. She lays two leathery-coated eggs at the end of it and incubates them by curling round them. After about a week the eggs hatch and the young feed on their mother's milk. It takes up to four months before the young are large enough to leave the burrow and feed on their own.

Duck-billed platypuses hunt underwater, scooping up insects, larvae and worms in their thick bill.

MARSUPIALS

Female marsupials have a pouch called a marsupium, and marsupials are often known as pouched mammals. The red kangaroo is one well known example. After the male and female kangaroos have mated, a fertilised egg develops inside the female to form a new animal. In 30–35 days the new animal is born and is known as a joey. Its eyes cannot open, it has no hair and only its front legs are well formed. The joey climbs through its mother's fur into the pouch and attaches itself to a teat to feed. After about six months the joey is fully formed and leaves the pouch but still returns there to rest. Just over a month later it leaves the pouch for the final time and grows into an adult.

Joeys often peer out from inside their mother's pouch.

PLACENTAL MAMMALS

The placental mammals are the largest group of mammals and include mice, monkeys, elephants, whales, cats, dogs, guinea pigs, horses and humans. Some mammals, such as humans and bats, usually only give birth to one young at a time. Other mammals, such as cats and mice, give birth to many more. After a mammal's egg is fertilised, it becomes attached to the uterus in the female by a blood-rich organ called a placenta. The fertilised egg develops into an embryo and, after a period of gestation, it is born. The baby mammal is fed on milk until it can find its own food.

A human embryo at seven weeks old. The placenta can be seen to the right of the picture.

INVESTIGATE

Use books and the Internet to find out about the different kinds of marsupial. On which continents are they found?

Kittens are usually ready to leave their mother at around 12 weeks old.

The life cycle of a human

Humans are placental mammals. Babies grow from a fertilised egg inside their mother's womb, where they develop for around nine months. The human life cycle is divided into seven periods when major changes in life take place.

This infant can sit up and move her head to look around at her surroundings.

INFANCY

Infancy lasts from birth to one year. For the first six months the baby is fed on milk. After that it starts to eat soft food. Between four months and six months old, an infant starts to sit up, roll over and hold its head up. The first or milk teeth begin to grow from about six months of age.

CHILDHOOD

Childhood lasts from one year up to 12 years of age. In the first year the child still has milk and soft food. After this, they can mostly eat an adult diet. First teeth fall out and are replaced by permanent teeth at around the age of six. Around the age of one, children start to stand up and then walk. They learn to use a cup and start to speak in sentences. By the end of childhood most children can read and perform complicated movements such as riding a bicycle.

Children need good control of their arms and legs to keep their balance on roller skates.

Adolescence is a time for building friendships and learning independence.

ADOLESCENCE

Adolescence lasts from the age of 12 to 18. In the early years of adolescence, puberty takes place. During this time the bodies of both sexes develop hair in the armpits and pubic region, and the sexual organs of both males and females develop. Males grow facial hair and their voice deepens; females develop breasts, wider hips and begin menstruation.

ADULTHOOD

Adulthood is from the age of 18 to around 55 when human bodies are at their strongest and fittest. Many people form partnerships and have children during this time. The body begins to lose some of its strength and fitness in the later stages of adulthood. The skin on the face may begin to wrinkle and hair may begin to turn grey.

MIDDLE AGE

Middle age is often considered to be from the age of 55 to 65. The body begins to weaken, but this can be slowed down by exercise. Wrinkles and grey hair become normal for many people. Body organs such as the heart may show signs of wear or disease and illnesses are now more common. The eyes can become less efficient and glasses may be needed for reading.

OLD AGE

During old age the muscles become smaller and weaker, bones become weaker and joints may be diseased. The ears may become less sensitive, leading to deafness. The body is less resistant to disease and takes longer to recover from injuries. Eventually failure of the body organs or disease leads to death, usually in the 80s or 90s, although some people can live to be over 100 years old!

INVESTIGATE

Compare the length of human life cycles to some other mammal life cycles, such as mice, rabbits, dogs, monkeys, elephants and whales. What do your results tell you?

People can stay active into old age by keeping in touch with friends.

Life cycles in a habitat

Stages in the life cycles of many of the plants and animals in a habitat are related to the four seasons of the year.

In spring a dragonfly nymph climbs out of the water and moults to become an adult.

WINTER

In the cold, wet, windy weather of winter, many living things hide away. The shoots of herbaceous plants have died back, but their roots and bulbs continue to survive under the soil. Some annual plants survive only in the seed stage. Many insects spend the winter hidden away at the egg and pupal stages, but some butterflies also hibernate as adults. Bats, which feed on flying insects, also hibernate. Amphibians such as frogs hibernate in mud, but birds, such as thrushes and finches, and mammals, such as deer and foxes, spend their winter searching for enough food to keep alive. None of them breed as the harsh winter weather would kill their young.

Bats spend winter in dry spaces in trees and caves.

SPRING

In spring the weather becomes warmer, less windy and drier. The shoots of herbaceous plants grow out of the soil. Insect eggs hatch into larvae. Pupae break open and the adults move away to find mates and breed. Frogs breed in ponds, their eggs hatch and the tadpoles develop into small adults by the end of summer. Birds that have spent the winter in the habitat pair up, build nests and rear young, while migrant birds return from warmer countries to begin breeding too. Mammals such as squirrels and foxes have their young and hide them away in nests and burrows to protect them.

SUMMER

In summer, mosses and ferns are ready to reproduce. They produce dust-like particles called spores that are carried away from the plant by the wind. Conifer trees make seeds in their cones that will open later to release them. Many flowering plants open their flowers for pollination, then begin to form fruits. Many birds may rear a second or third brood, while young mammals continue to grow and learn the skills from their parents that will help them survive alone.

In summer, many flowers open. Butterflies feed on the nectar to give them energy to fly, find a mate and breed.

AUTUMN

In the autumn the weather becomes cooler, windier and wetter again. By then flowering plants have made all the food they need to produce their fruits and prepare them for dispersal. The winged parachute fruits of the maple and willow herb are dispersed by the strong autumn winds. Succulent fruits such as berries are eaten by birds as they build up food stores in their bodies to survive the winter. The birds also help in the life cycles of trees by dispersing their berry seeds unharmed in their bird droppings. Migrant insect-eating birds return to warmer countries for the winter and frogs and their young prepare to hibernate in mud once more for the winter.

Some birds such as geese migrate between two habitats each year to avoid harsh winter weather and to find a place in which to rear their young.

INVESTIGATE

Take photos or make sketches of a local habitat, such as a woodland, during the different seasons. What changes can you see?

Life cycle journeys

The life cycle of many living things involves a journey. Plants remain rooted to the soil but their seed and fruits make journeys, aided mainly by the wind and animals. Animals can make journeys at almost any time in their life cycle, as these examples from the ocean show.

PLANKTON

The plankton in the upper waters of seas and oceans contains billions of plants and animals. The plants belong to a group called algae and spend their time in the plankton where they simply drift with the currents. The animals also drift, but this is only part of their journey. Most of the animals in plankton arrive there as eggs. The eggs float out from the seashore or up from the sea bed where they have been laid.

INVERTEBRATES IN PLANKTON

When invertebrate eggs in plankton hatch they form larvae which are very different to the adults. The larvae have adaptations such as bands of hairs or long arms to help keep them in the plankton. In time the larvae leave the plankton, land on the shore or sea bed and change into adults.

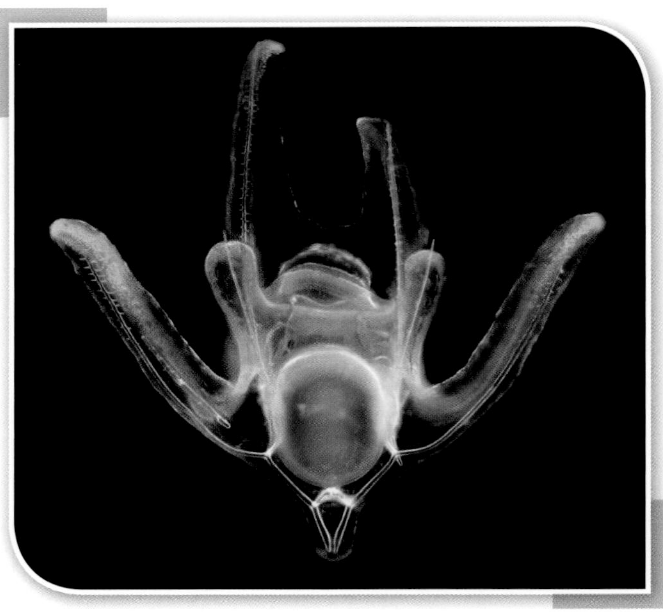

Starfish larvae have long arms to stop them sinking quickly in the water.

FISH IN THE PLANKTON.

Many marine fish, such as the tuna, lay eggs which float up into the plankton. The larvae that hatch from the eggs bring the egg yolks with them and use them as food to form their bodies. A fully formed tiny fish is called a juvenile. It feeds on other animals in the plankton. In time, some young fish such as sardines join other adults swimming in shoals in the same habitat – the upper waters of the sea. Others, such as plaice, which live on the sea floor, will make the journey down to their new habitat.

When a plaice turns into a juvenile, both its eyes move to one side of its head so the fish can lay down sideways on the sea floor to hide.

MIGRATIONS

Some animals migrate from one habitat to another, then go back to the first habitat to complete their life cycle.

SALMON

Salmon eggs are laid in the gravelly bottoms of rivers high in the hills. When the eggs hatch the young fish stay in the river for some time, often as long as a few years. When they reach a certain size called a smolt, they leave the river and swim out into the sea where they may live for a few years, feeding on krill, sardine and young herring. The fully grown salmon return to the river and to the place where their parents bred. They find mates and breed there too.

Salmon rushing upriver to breed.

MARINE TURTLES

Female marine turtles lay their eggs in a hole on a sandy beach and then bury them. When the young hatch they climb out of the hole and rush down the beach and into the sea where they will be safe from predators on the seashore, such as crabs and sea birds. They spend many years at sea, travelling thousands of kilometres, but when they are ready to breed they return to the waters near the beach where they hatched to find a mate. The female then climbs up the beach and lays her eggs, before returning out to sea to feed.

INVESTIGATE

Find out more about the migration of the European and Alaskan salmon and the green, loggerhead and leatherback turtle.

Newly-hatched turtles rush for the sea to avoid hungry predators on the beach.

Studying life cycles

People have studied plants and animals from ancient times. Over the years, their detailed observations, investigations and presentations have greatly increased our knowledge of many plant and animal life cycles.

RUDOLF JAKOB CAMERARIUS (1665–1721)

Rudolf Jakob Camerarius was a German botanist and physician who lived in the late 17th and early 18th century. He took charge of the botanical gardens in Tübigen in Germany and made investigations into reproductive systems of the flowers of mulberry trees, a group of plants called spurges and the spinach plant. He identified the male and female reproductive parts of a plant as the anther (male) and pistil (female). He also discovered that pollen was needed for seeds to form.

GILBERT WHITE (1720–1793)

Gilbert White was an ornithologist and naturalist who lived in the 18th century in Hampshire in England. He observed and recorded when plants came into leaf, when they flowered and formed fruit and when tree leaves changed colour and fell. He also recorded when butterflies left their pupae, frogs spawned, tadpoles hatched, birds sang, nested and reared their young. He wrote a book called *The Natural History of Selbourne*, which was published in 1789. His observations in the book inspired a great many other people to take up observing plants and animals in their habitats, which eventually led to the science of ecology.

Gilbert White made many observations on the life cycle of swallows.

This male stickleback is helping to build a nest (bottom right) by spitting sand.

NIKOLAAS TINBERGEN (1907–1988)

Nikolaas Tinbergen was born in the Netherlands in 1907. As a boy he caught fish called sticklebacks in ditches near his home and set them up in an aquarium to study them. Later in adult life he studied their behaviour in more detail. He described the way in which the male stickleback builds a nest, attracts females, guards the eggs and looks after the young until they can look after themselves.

DAVID ATTENBOROUGH (1926–)

David Attenborough is a renowned British naturalist, writer and presenter of TV programmes about plants and animals in which the details of life cycles are featured. In one of his films he shows the life cycles of the 17-year cicada. This is an insect related to the grasshopper, which hatches from the egg as a nymph and spends 17 years underground feeding on tree root sap. At the end of this time the nymphs climb out of the soil, moult into adults, breed and die. David has used his writing and presenting skills to bring life cycle discoveries to people all over the world.

David Attenborough has visited habitats all over the world.

This adult cicada has spent 17 years as a nymph and is ready to breed.

INVESTIGATE

Use books and the Internet to find out more about the work of famous naturalists such as Alexander von Humboldt, John Muir and Jane Goodall.

Glossary

Algae – a plant with no leaves or stems that grows in water or damp places.

Annual – a plant which completes its life cycle in a year.

Asexual reproduction – the reproduction of a plant or organism without the formation and fusion of gametes. The resulting offspring is identical to its one parent.

Biennial – a plant which completes its life cycle in two years.

Botanist – a scientist who studies the structure and life cycles of plants.

Brood – the young of a pair of birds that hatched at the same time.

Carnivore – an animal that only eats animals.

Community – a group of people living together in an area such as a neighbourhood or all the plants and animals living in a habitat.

Embryo – the developing body of an animal in an egg or uterus.

Ephemeral – a plant which completes its life cycle in a few weeks.

Fertilisation – the joining together of a male and female gamete to produce a fertilised ovule in a plant and fertilised egg in an animal.

Gamete – a sex cell, it contains half the instructions to make a new plant or animal.

Germinate – when as seed sprouts to produce a root and shoot.

Gestation period – the time from fertilisation of a placental mammal egg until the young is born.

Gill – a part of the body that an aquatic animal uses for breathing in water.

Herbivore – an animal that only eats plants.

Incubation – the process in which eggs are kept warm by either parent sitting on them.

Larva – a stage in the life cycle of many insects. It may also be called the caterpillar, rub or maggot.

Mating – a process in which the male sex cells called sperm are transferred to the female sex cells called the eggs or ova. Following mating a sperm fuses with an egg in a process called fertilisation to form a cell, which will grow into a new animal.

Menstruation – a monthly release of blood from the reproductive organs of females who are not pregnant.

Moulting (in birds) – the process of losing old feathers and growing new ones.

Moulting (in insects) – a process in which an insect breaks out of its old skin so that it can grow larger.

Naturalist – a person who studies plants and animals in their habitats – often as a hobby.

Nymph – a stage in the life cycles of some insects where it looks like a miniature adult.

Ornithologist – a person who studies birds in their habitat, noting their behaviour and the arrival and departure of migrants.

Perennial – a plant which takes many years to complete its life cycle.

Placenta – the attachment of the embryo to the uterus which transfers food and oxygen from the mother's blood to the embryo and transfers wastes from the embryo's blood to the mother.

Predator – an animal that eats other animals.

Pubic region – the area of skin at the top of the legs in male and female adult humans.

Pupa – the stage in many insect life cycles where the insect changes from a larva to an adult. The pupa is sometimes called the chrysalis or cocoon.

Reed – a water plant with a tall thin shoot.

Stickleback – a small fish found in ponds and streams which has three or more spines sticking up on its back.

Termite – an insect similar to an ant that lives in tropical regions of the world.

Uterus – an organ in the female mammal in which embryos develop.

Index

ABOUT THIS BOOK

This aim of this book is to provide information and enrichment for the topic of Life Cycles in the Upper Key Stage 2 UK Science Curriculum. There are five lines of scientific enquiry. By reading the book the children are making one of them – research using secondary sources. The text is supported by simple investigations the reader can make to experience what has been described. Many of these investigations are simply illustrative to reinforce what has been read and practise observational skills, but the following investigations are also examples of types of scientific enquiry. Grouping and classifying: pages 5, 7, 9 ; Observing over time: pages 11, 25; Researching using secondary sources (extension): pages 13, 17, 19, 21, 23, 27; Comparative test: pages 15, 23.